I AM BECOMING
A SELECTION OF POETRY FROM PROPAGANDA

humble beast.

Author: Jason Petty
Executive Producer: Thomas J. Terry
Edited by Carissa Arend & Jason Petty
Cover and layout by Anthony M. Benedetto for Humble Beast
All photos by Kristopher Squints - www.squintfoto.com
Project management by Paul Barger for Stumptown Management
Production management by Rene Garzona for Humble Beast
Printed by Bang Printing

Copyright © 2015 by Jason Petty / Humble Beast Records
All rights reserved. No part of this publication may be reproduced, distributed, or transmitted in any form or by any means, including photocopying, recording, or other electronic or mechanical methods, without the prior written permission of the publisher, except in the case of brief quotations embodied in critical reviews and certain other noncommercial uses permitted by copyright law. For permission requests, write to the publisher, addressed "Attention: Permissions Coordinator," at the email below.

Humble Beast Publishing, Portland, Oregon 2015
ISBN 978-0-692-50847-3

Ordering Information:
Quantity sales. Special discounts are available on quantity purchases by corporations, associations, ministries and others. For details, contact the publisher at info@humblebeast.com
Orders by U.S. trade bookstores and wholesalers. Please contact Humble Beast:
Tel: (503) 213-3416; or visit www.humblebeast.com.

Printed in the United States of America

Contributors:
Amanda Rameriz - Johnnyswim
Lecrae Moore - Reach Records
Bj Thompson- Build a Better Us
Eric Turbedsky - Sovereign Grace OC
Cameron Strang- Relevant Magazine
Jamie Tworkowski - To Write Love On Her Arms
Leonce Crump - Renovation Church
Amisho Baraka- Forth district / Lions and Liars

TABLE OF CONTENTS

1. DEDICATION
2. RESPONSE BY AMANDA RAMIREZ

CHAPTER 1

3. I AM BECOMING...SELF AWARE
4. SELF AWARE
5. IT'S COMPLICATED
6. DON'T LISTEN TO ME
7. YOU MOCK ME
8. MY CAREER
9. I AIN'T GOT AN ANSWER
10. REPONSE BY SHO BARAKA
11. MY NEXT RECORD
12. SONG OF THE CITY
13. ON THE OTHER HAND
14. COMO SE DICE
15. BEAUTIFUL PAIN

CHAPTER 2

16. I AM BECOMING...MORE ASTUTE
17. MORE ASTUTE
18. DEAR BORED OF EDUCATION
19. RESPONSE BY LECRAE
20. THREE CORD BOND
21. RESPONSE BY BJ THOMPSON
22. STRETCH MARKS
23. WARM WORDS
24. PRECIOUS PURITANS
25. RESPONSE BY ERIC TURBEDSKY
26. FORGIVE ME FOR ASKING
27. THEY REALLY NOT SO DIFFERENT
28. JESUS WASN'T A COMMUTER
29. THE HEALTHY DON'T NEED DOCTORS

CHAPTER 3

30. I AM BECOMING...RESOLVED
31. RESOLVED
32. CONQUER
33. RESPONSE BY REV. LEONCE B. CRUMP JR.
34. I STILL DON'T SEE IT
35. JPEG
36. NEED YOU MORE THAN EVER
37. REDEFINE CUTTER
38. SINEMA
39. YOU GOTTA DIG
40. RESPONSE BY JAMIE TWORKOWSKI
41. HANDS OFF THE BRAKES
42. WHAT IF YOU KNEW?

CHAPTER 4

43. I AM BECOMING...AND ALWAYS WILL BE
44. I'M SO DONE WASTING WORDS
45. AND NOW
46. PERFECT PICTURE
47. BE PRESENT
48. RESPONSE BY CAMERON STRANG
49. ALPHA MALE
50. BECAUSE
51. TOO CREATIVE
52. TELL ME YOURS

Caterpillars who fall in love with their cocoons...Lose.

1

DEDICATION

To my Soul: I prolly could made your middle name Poetry. I was performing poems about race when I found out you existed, was writing this poetry book during your cocooning. And your mother's refusal of even an IV, wanting to feel every ache, a privilege only given to the yang of humanity. And if yin had any sense, it would envy. That's poetry. Her love for her Incan ancestral instincts, her craving to share in the pain of her foremothers in your delivery. That's Poetry. It's good to know that one day you too will wield that type of power. You peeked the tip of your head out of your past. The safety of your personal Mother Earth. My wife. She was no longer one pregnant woman. You were two people. That's Alma, that's Soul. Such a simple idea. But the image sealed it for me. You're two people. Not one person with a ball of tissue festering inside. You are not an inconvenience. You are my maturity. You are my time. You make me in no hurry. There are not enough feels or fears. You are my Egypt, my evidence that we were once superior and royal and flawed and helpless. And will crack the pavement of time for all. Our posterity to envy. You are why.

To my Moon: You were a packaged deal. What learning to love means. You are the picture of what God does for outsiders. We share no DNA but identical passion for yo' Mamma. You are not an inconvenience. You are not a stepdaughter. You are my humility. You are, in an ironic twist, my mirror. My lessons. You two were tattooed on my fingertips, by archangels with ink extracted from lilac on Jupiter. See, you ain't know Jupiter has beautiful gardens on it. But God shrouded it with poisonous clouds because the dirty hands of man's 10 year plans and life goals would soil its beauty. You can't touch the ink of the future. Its pedals are too much for you. Your potential is too much for me. These words are beneath you. My hopes for you are beneath you. My poems are beneath you. You are my play on words.
My apprehension. My second guess.
My insecurity. My pyramid. My Mayan temple. My reminder that pre-Columbian us was amazing, yet post is no different. You two. My Sol. My soul. My moon. My Luna. My daughters. This is yours.

2

RESPONSE BY AMANDA RAMIREZ

Propaganda gave words to the beautiful ache and honor I feel as a new mother in his poem to his daughters. They made me feel known in my new parenthood. My son has already lived five months, and I grapple daily with how to describe his birth and the incessantly growing adoration I have for him. These poems say what I've so often felt over the last few months and haven't been able to articulate. I too chose to birth my son naturally, a decision I never thought twice about and regularly defended to people who felt it was either needlessly reckless or self-indulgent. What they didn't understand was the importance for me to be an active and full participant in bringing my son into this world. It wasn't wasted energy. I changed with each contraction.
My identity morphed with each push.
Finally, after hours of labor, he made it official and the process had fully transformed me.
I became a mother breath by breath. The pain was nothing. It wasn't even pain, it was an honor.

It was a privilege. It was just as Prop said…it was poetry. Fear couldn't keep me from it, and even my greatest hopes couldn't have prepared me for it. It's so beautiful to see Propaganda echo this feeling as a father witnessing his wife lead his daughter so valiantly earthside. It's all a bit mind-boggling and heartbreaking in the best way! Regardless of how our children come to us, parenthood is so truly "the picture of what God does" for us who were all once outsiders. Loving my child in full recognition that he is both fragile and royal has made me understand the weight of Heaven's love for me in a way I never imagined. Our kids, our little temples, our ultimate heritage – they are greater than our hopes and greater than our fears. I hear Prop say "my hopes for you are beneath you." Yes. I feel this everyday. With awe, joy, and holy fear, I feel it everyday.

- Amanda Ramirez JOHNNYSWIM

3

I AM BECOMING...SELF AWARE

In my childhood, I was fascinated by four things: the ThunderCats, graffiti, black history, and Regan Revere. Regan was the other black kid at my preschool. I had a huge crush on her – haven't seen her since 3rd grade. I dated a girl in college who said she went to high school with Regan. She said Regan joined the Peace Corps after they graduated and moved to India. It's amazing how things turn out. I wanted to draw cartoons when I grew up or be a stand-up comedian. Somehow the images I wanted to draw became word paintings. And the graffiti murals covering the LA river that I desperately wanted to be a part of got traded for memory murals. I was fortunate enough to fall in love with hip hop during the era of the mid 80s to early 90s. With the backdrop of a father who made sure I understood and appreciated my heritage, I was able to connect the dots from Fats Domino to Chuck D, from The Winans to Eazy-E, Negro spirituals to New Jack Swing. Rap, poetry, history, faith, and salvation were always connected to me. I think I'm seeing that more and more these days. These poems are almost like the dots for you to play connect the dots with. Only the good Lord knows what the image will be. As for me, all I know is I am becoming.

4

SELF AWARE

They started me wit' Beat Street, sweet peas, and Sunday school. Told me 'bout Noah's Ark and how Herk was cool. Taught me that black was a blessing and an honor, the truth of Sojourner – here's a book on Nat Turner. Pops rented videos on sandwich heros, hipped to my heritage like Miss Jane Pittman. Meanwhile, church services – I could never miss them. Mama made me take notes to see if I was listening. Lived among the Mexicans, so I never did the "crip thang." Instead, they gave me cans to write my name up on the bricks thang. Big sister house danced, her guy friends wrote raps, and Mama saw her son get addicted to the boom bap. All the while, God's training me to hear His voice, because only He knew I would be a choice. Tagger slash rapper, son of a Black Panther, we got high hopes for him: "He gon be a pastor!" Do I run wit' the church boys, backpacks, or thugs? Funny, Lord's answer was all of the above. Son, stay cool; son, stay in school; son, learn the Word of God; you were born to rule. My love, my color, my Lord, my God. My school of the hard knocks, high hats, and fat caps. But that's what I'm about: return of the juke joint, color of your rag homeboy is a mute point. Lift up your glass and let it blast from the jukebox! Come on back home. We were born to get hot.

5

IT'S COMPLICATED

We are our own demise. I am becoming procrastination. Reckless, sexist, crooked. Confused. You are so often wrong about you and uoeno. We have self-identified as particleboard, paper mâché, duct taped. And we are wrong. And right. And confused. It's complicated. But so is a star. A flower. A quasar. A friendship. A marriage. May we become a refuge for the complicated. As for me, well, I'll zip up my emotions into this dusty duffel bag I've aptly named poetry and I'll be on my merry way as soon as my pride turns me loose. I'll unmangle the last morsel of manhood I could muster. Ma'am, I seem to have misplaced my confidence. Last place I've seen it, it was right at the altar of your love. It's complicated. I am becoming... complicated. We may scratch ourselves raw to erase the image we were made in. Smoke, snort, sex, or drown out the silence. We may waste our savings on makeovers to rhinoplasty our daddy's nose away. But no nip, no tuck can cut away the sense of obligation. We are becoming what we are not. But what we are is inescapable. You are a masterpiece fighting to be a silly selfie with a hideous filter. You are handmade heavens and calligraphy slumming it among papyrus fonts. You are a perfect and eternal poet – laureate – complete works with a laundry list of identity issues. Sometimes our plumbing don't match our urges. Your femininity forged a force field that protects your posterity. Your masculinity musters up moxey to conquer mountains for your family. You are rightful heir to not just a kingdom, but a universe and you have your father's eyes. Stop acting like a traitor. You are revelation revealed. You are pyramid constructors, conductors, conduits of lightning. At the same time you speak, you breathe arsenic carcinogenic, causes car sickness. These scars are our witness. To love hard is hard living. But it's life. It's what you are. It's what you will be. And it's complicated. But then again, so are stars, childbirth, parenting, us.

6

DON'T LISTEN TO ME

I'm not delusional. This most likely might be your first experience with me. Greetings, my name is Propaganda. I wrote my first rap in '93. Simply put, fire-baptized battle rapper who's heavily influenced by folk music and found creative freedom in poetry. The combo is strange, I know. Let this one bake your noodle. I'm a son of a Black Panther with a Mexican spouse and Caucasian best friends. My writing tone, now, is not one that offers you neat little bows to tie all your problems up with. I've learned enough to know I don't know that much. I know God became a man to save us, and we still can't explain the pyramids. I know the ancient Mayans and Egyptian astronomers had a far greater understanding of outer space than we do. I know academia is so drunk on arrogance and racism that they'd rather credit these accomplishments to aliens than admit we are not the smartest civilization to ever live. I know I really love my wife, my daughter, and mangos. And for some reason, folks find it illogical to think that a perfectly designed universe screams of a designer. I know sarcasm is really the only time most people tell the truth. I know chilaquiles and In-N-Out will be served in Heaven. And it's a much better decision to shut your mouth when you don't know what you're talking about than to validate what everyone already thinks of you. I know color theory very well. I have a degree in Illustration and Intercultural Studies and a teaching credential, yet I rap for a living. Let that sink in. Apparently I don't know that much: just the gospel and good hip hop. I'm a pretty simple dude. All I got is my All. And I promise you, I'll give you that. Lower standards will lower the culture. The Roman empire was destroyed because of lowered standards and moral decay. You know, they murdered each other and fed their own to lions for entertainment. Humans left to their own devices seem to be hopelessly selfish and bent on their own destruction. Seems like unless a power greater than us captures our hearts, nothing will change that trajectory. Wealth, knowledge, and success seem to just feed the beast. But don't listen to me, we just met. What do I know?

7

YOU MOCK ME

And I asked you be a symbol of the strength I was once given, yet you mock me. Oh, so much mockery. I placed so much confidence in the lessons I swear you taught me, yet you mock me. You taunt me about glory days. You say my best is behind me. You just bring up old stuff. Our relationship is so unhealthy, so codependent. You cut me down. You blame me. I blame me. But I'm a man I don't crack I show no emotion, right? I do just like my daddy did and his daddy too and I bury you. Well, I built a mausoleum with a storage unit attached to it just for you. I've grown so very weary of failing at making you stay there. Why won't you stay there? I hate it when you show up at my functions. You're so pompous with not an ounce of shame. You almost ruined my marriage. You mock me. I tried to upgrade the way I speak and raise my daughter but every time my mouth opens all I hear is my father. Same foolish pride and pitfalls that he installed leaks through my pores like, "Poor me." It's so annoying. I placed so much faith in you and you let me down. I see my own eyes as an 8-year-old when I correct her. Why won't you go away? You smirk as you chase me. You're a coy Helen of Troy who toys with emotions. Feeble-brained boys like me fall for it every time. You mock me. I'll probably do my best to convince you that I'm the victim – you just don't believe me. You insist you are me. I've ran and ran, yet your stride is identical. Every step I took, your foot fit right in it. I can't shake you. Why can't I shake you? You are my past. Why won't you stay there? You are the pain that guides us. The string that ties us. The coincidence that proves to us God's existence. The joy I misplaced. Beautiful mistakes. My scarlet thread. My crimson cord.

8

MY CAREER

My career. Where the most intimate, personal, and special moments between a man and his wife that can only be truly appreciated for the two it was made for is chewed up and spit out in the form of a new poem, or song, or tweet. And y'all eat it up. And my kids need to. My poor wife married a surveillance camera with anger problems. Don't judge me. You carry moment-killers in your pockets too. My career. Got me hating to take pictures and at the same time terrified for the day y'all won't want one. Exhausting and exhilarating. Beating the drum that my life is not my own, yet when y'all treat me like I belong to you, I long for the hotel room. This is not real life. Yet it's the one I'm living. Tour buses that drop me off at daycare. I'm just tryin' to get my daughter to flush the toilet when she's done. My career. Where total strangers know my secrets and have convos wit' me like we share a 12-step class. Where people believe Instagram comments and threats of unfollowing will make my pride a bitter side dish with dinner. I welcome your thoughts. I stand before you. In a strange twist of fate, I found my prayers need prayer. My tears, a good scrubbing. My repentance, need to do just that. My career.

9

I AIN'T GOT AN ANSWER

When it's apparent that you have failed as a parent: too busy trying to pay rent, now what? Homie, long gone are the days. You're not taking your lil' big head to ASYO scrimmages, no more football practice, little league, movie nights. You're driving to his cute lil' puppy love girlfriend's doctor's appointment. She's got a date with the sonogram and your boy is officially a statistic. Now what? Your lil' big head – he's barely sprouting peach fuzz. He wanna be just like you; he wanna write poetry. He feels akin to buffalo soldiers. You chuckle. We live in suburbs. I worked too hard for you to not struggle. You don't know what you're talking about. You soon find that socioeconomic status does nothing for his skin color. To them, he's just a well-dressed coon whose parents got lucky. He's the butt of subliminal racist jokes, like his friends refer to rap as jungle jive. They see him and go, "Yo homie, yo! Y'all talk like that." He's checked out. He's found other outlets. His good grades don't fix his depraved brain. He believes the gospel of young money. Yolo. As your mamma drops you off at the mall, remember as you scope em Dunks out, every bite you take of that Number 1 Animal Style is a bite you stole out of your daughter's tummy. Them Dunks is about a month of diapers and food you wear on your feet. This is your fault, your job, your responsibility. You get mad at your parents for not giving you 20 bucks, homie, it's your turn. Now what? When it's apparent that you have failed as a parent, cancel quinceañeras. Lil' mama's finna be one. He's scrolling through his iPhone's unopened emails. How many daughter's hugs did I not reply to? You ain't lyin' to me and I know the song you're singing That promise ring was cute but it was really for the parents. She ain't savin' it for marriage and never had plans to. Now she's in a fetal position carrying a fetus. Your worldview officially left the philosophical and is laying on your living room considering abortion. Them 8 grade boys is texting naked pictures of your daughter to each other, now what? Baby girl, them is your panties posted on his Facebook. Now what? This is your fault. And I ain't got an answer. Dad, sit in it. Stew in it. Soak in it. You failed. You'd better get it together. She needs you more than ever.

10

RESPONSE BY SHO BARAKA

Let's jump right into it! I prayed God's will be done. Whether I understood it or not, it's the conventional thing to say. When I recite these petitions I rarely think that HE will actually proceed to do what HE thinks is best for me. I often figure HE knows what I think to be the preferred alternative and follows through with a genie-esque compliance. I say things like, "Your will be done," just to complete my Protestant due diligence. Am I willing to surrender all to uncertainty? As a parent, I know I prayed these idioms while actually asking God to sign off on the agenda I had set for my future in parenting. But then reality hit. It was the question for which I had no answer. How could a loving God place on me the burden of raising a child with autism? What is autism? Is this genetic? Should we have more children? Will my son be able to speak, use the restroom, or engage in public activities without me being embarrassed? Will he know God in a way that is acceptable to my church family? How will this affect my marriage? Will we have to put him in special needs housing one day? Who will take care of him when we die? I didn't have an answer. I still don't have an answ to much of this. My father was my hero at a young age. He was also a man who was deeply flawed. However, I was too busy being consumed with his presence in my life to be worried about his shortcomings. He tried to stick around even though my parents were losing love for one another. Eventually their selfishness championed their desire to raise kids together. Many years later my dad would go from a consistent visitor to an apparition. I went three years without speaking to him. I accepted that I would grow into my teenage years without having my father around. One day an unfamiliar car pulled up to my house. My father was the lone passenger. He proceeded to take me on a two-hour cruise around the city. With every turn of the car there was a tear falling from his eye, symbolizing an apology for his selfish ways. He confessed his sins to me like I was his priest and his car was the confessional. After all that, all I can remember is, "My dad is back!" I was happy to have my father back in my life. I may have checked out 30 minutes into the spill once I got confirmation that he was committed to me again. I've learned a very important truth about that day. My father needed that 2 hour speech. He was a better parent because of that moment. I believe that speech was more for him than it was for me. Guilt and shame makes the soul heavy. Repentance and confession makes the soul joyful. If there is one thing I have learned, it is that this process isn't really about my son. This process is really about me. I've learned so much about myself without my son even critiquing my parenting. Autism is the vehicle that has lead me to repent and confess my selfish ways. I've learned about how impatient I am. How hypocritical I can be. How prideful I am. How much anger I have in me. I've found jealousy in the deep corners of my heart. I've learned how a parent can place their own insecurities on their kid, how they use their children as a measurement of success. I am guilty of all these things. Once I understood the envy and frustration I harbored, I became a better man for it. My son was the law that showed me my shortcomings. I have a new palette to work from. It's a palette based on grace and forgiveness. My previous work was constructed from false perceptions and people-pleasing. I've learned that fatherhood isn't based on performance. The love for my son is not affected by how well he performs a task. I have failed many times and I will continue to fail. He will fall short in his performance. His value is in his position as my son and not in his production. He is mine and I am his. As cliché as it sounds, my affection for him hasn't changed since the day he was a alien-like confirmation in an ultrasound examination. I still don't have the answers, but I know a merciful God has given me the perfect person to humble me. I say to all parents, no matter the set of issues in your house, demonstrate the Christian life in every way. It does you no good to think poisonously but act healthy. My poisonous thoughts would soon expose me and demand allegiance. However, I'm glad I eventually found grace again, just as bright as the first day of salvation. My wife and I once asked an older wiser couple about advice on how to raise children with special needs, and they replied, "Love each other and try to live a long time. They will need that." We all have different problems but it's the same problem. All I can do is "Be Present" as my man Propaganda says. I know that parenting is one of the only institutions that failing while being present is still appreciated. My soul is less heavy now that I dealt with my guilt and shame. So I guess my answer is "Love and live long enough to make an impact."

- *Sho Baraka*
FORTH DISTRICT / LIONS AND LIARS

11

MY NEXT RECORD

My next record makes no mention of champagne, strippers, or haters. It will not compare rap to crack. There will be no stories of me being caught cheating. I've never sold a drug. I will not refer to any jail time for the purpose of credibility on the mic because I was never locked up. My next record will not only speak of mistakes I've made in the past tense. Although I have been redeemed, I am far from perfect. My next record will not speak of money in any way, shape, or form greater than a means to an end. I will not speak of women in terms of their parts. I will not exalt hip hop as the answer to all of societal woes. I will not constantly tell you how dope I am. My hope is it will be painfully obvious. My next record will not melt your face off literally, but figuratively. It will be biblically sound and awkwardly awesome. People who disagree with its worldview will like it. People who don't like hip hop will like it. It will offend you. It might inspire you. My next record will not sound like or outsell Lecrae's record, Drake's record, J. Cole's, or Wiz Khalifa's. I will not say crunk or swag at any point. My daughter will love it yet still like Miley Cyrus more. I will pray she grows out of that stage quickly. My album will make the headliner uncomfortable. There will be battle raps, apologetics, and exegesis. There will be references you won't get if you've never read a Bible or lived on the West Coast, specifically Los Angeles. Or West Covina. There will be no profanity but a lot of big words, multiple word plays, and political statements that black people normally don't make. It will honor my people's achievements and ridicule our ridiculous glorification of pimps and obsession with ignorance. It will attack black church practices that are clearly unbiblical and poke fun at activists that only rep at poetry venues and backpackers whose sole purpose is to prove they are the most underground. My next record will not change the world, but it will touch it. My next record will be thoroughly and consistently, with all my ability – so help me Lord – excellent.

Press on culture instead of being pressured by it.

12

THE SONG OF THE CITY

They say the city sings a song. And you can't help but sing along. And I'll be looking in their eyes like, "I'm sorry, you're dead wrong." We came from birth sinning and from very meager beginnings where all we had was spam and an interceding grandma. Tried to read the Word but didn't understand the grammar 'til His grace came and gave me a new brain. You cannot tell me that poverty is bigger than sovereignty. We lived in the same projects as you, lived right next you, dodged the same bullets, even spent time in the "burbs." That's my word. When you're born off Alondra with drugs and money launderers, now a husband and father, that is proof that a God loves you. We chose not to slang and that gave me much more bravery than those OGs would ever give me credit for. The road was so lonely and we had God only. And fools would creep by slowly like, "What up, homie!" But steady wins the race. Open your ears, y'all been hustling for years. It sounds like you're grinding gears! Stripping up your clutch and ironically it's automatic. I'm gonna literally drive by your drive-bys. You are not your hood, homie. It did not make you. Look, we are proof you don't have to conform. That road was so lonely but you cannot tell me it's impossible to exit that mosh pit scarless. You don't have to sing along. She came from birth sinning and very meager beginnings where she shared a bed with her sister 'til 18. First out of high school, first out of college, childhood was a nightmare, somehow she got out of there. A simple girl, beautiful, complex. Her complexion is quite similar to Incan or Mayan. Her speaking reminds me of my time in east Los – reformed Chola Loca. Working on her PhD like, "You think I'm plain?! Man, I'm from HP, homie, by way of Acapulco!" It would crush someone lesser, elementary school off of Fir and Manchester. Thank God He blessed her. You are not your hood, homie. It did not make you.

13

ON THE OTHER HAND

This is Citizen Aim-inspired, proclaiming the Lord Sire 'til his lungs expired! Literally. That's what you do wIth your own organs. Mutiny! For every person who was forced to pick whether they were visual or auditory learners, a mic or black book burners. Broad-brush victims with a vicious vendetta to prove that they are not them. I got you, every less road traveler. This is what love tastes like, like…if you could only hear my sketchbook, with drums front and center like they're starving for attention. So tempted to wax cold and grow calluses.
God grant us a blessing in honor of Oscar Grant. My people's hearts have gone granite. Granted, I expected them to. I apologize, unsung ones.
Your stories are not told much – it don't make for good headlines. No one cares about the lefties. But on the other hand, we bring art from the other hand, powerful brushstrokes of the Son of Man. But on the other hand.

14

COMO SE DICE

It feels so uncomfortable. I'm so used to a ton of bull, so when it feels real it feels unbelievable. It feels like walking hand in hand with emo bands, bangs over my eyes and girl pants. It feels so God-breathed – don't tease me – an unclear move of His spirit, believe me. A struggle because my own thoughts can be deceiving. A seething deception with evil inceptions but it feels so right, which ironically don't feel right because it ain't never felt right. You feel me, right? It's like trading brains with Maxwell or a John Legend type of fellow. It feels like overdrafts, because them kicks is bad and she's gotta have them and she ain't asking for them. It feels like one of my organs were stolen so when we're apart I feel un-whole and broken. And my life was gold, you could ask the homie Holden. He believed in me when no one came to see me.

It feels like the future is far greater than I could have ever imagined, like, how did this happen? It feels like 5 miles outside of Cannon, or Harriet Tubman when she first saw the Mason–Dixon line that de-marks our freedom. It feels like freedom, like it's impossible for anything anywhere to be more important than this moment. It feels like I might bite some incubus lyrics, infinitely interesting. Like all around her fades into duotones and she remains a vibrant CMYK. What more can I say? She is soul – esta mi alma. She is my moon – esta mi luna. I can't find the words, at least in my language. I don't how to say this. Let's try in Spanglish. Como se dice? Some things can't even be said in poetry, but I'll give it a shot. You are what I'm not, what I wish to be, let me find a simile. Como se dice?

15

BEAUTIFUL PAIN

Put it up, them bruises are beautiful. These key ingredients are beautiful. Like cheekbone birthmarks in the shapes of roses or third-degree burns that retired firemen earn. What a privilege. Like Auntie's not embarrassed of her scars, breast-less but breathless. That's pain. Like handcrafted scars, a tapestry of bruises. It's beautiful mutilation, like branding and tattoos. That's pain. Like ancient pagan practices of scarification, it damages skin horribly but them marks demark royalty. That's pain. Marred in the Potter's hands, that's pain. Off on purpose, but if you don't know your purpose you might feel worthless. Like hearing the buzz of the motor as the needle digs deep, shoving the ink further, forcing in the permanence. Made again another, bottling up my tears, 'til the day that we rise. Toss your arthritis-filled knuckles to the sky. That's pain. They're beautiful, like Hail Mary full of grace. She was proud of her stretch marks, how her skin expanded to bring forth the Son of Man. That's pain. But it's beautiful, like villages before we discovered them. It's beautiful, like Grandmama singing in memory of Dr. Martin Luther King, see. We used to stay off of Martin Luther King, homie, I'm from South Central and that's beautiful. You're looking at a lastborn rightful heir to the throne, son of a nobody with poverty in my bones, and that's beautiful. We never had nothing but nothing, what's up. It kept my belly full of the stuff the rich were missing and that's beautiful. Thank God for the tax return that got us up out of there, that's beautiful. So in honor of Jimi Hendrix, I string life's instrument backwards and choose to play the back, because in the Word, the last is first and that's beautiful.

16

I AM BECOMING...MORE ASTUTE

I got the ticket, the jaywalking ticket. Because I didn't cross the street fast enough, a residential street right behind my school. I was walking with Brandon and Ronnie home after school and we were crossing the street diagonally. Apparently, it took me, only me, too long to get across the street. I think I took too long because of the two "onlies" I possessed. I was the only one that got a ticket, and I was the only black kid. As a person of color, you are never really and truly prepared for the realization that the country you live in doesn't necessarily have your best interests in mind, nor has it ever. But there is a long list of people who came before you that fought to give you a better life. Then there's the point that you realize you're supposed to be on that list.

17

MORE ASTUTE

The cry of a desperate mother, Daddy is at his wit's end. Granny don't know what to do with her kid's kids. Ritalin is failing him, 10th grade he's failing it. Youth pastor bailed on him, teachers can't riddle him. Po-po can't find him, out wit' his cousins. He's on the same streets that his tios and primos were killed in, hustling is built in. To whom is he listening? Not you, he's lost all controls of what influences him. Him got his eye on her, her in many mini skirts, desperate for attention and showing them curves work. Send her to live wit' Auntie, she stay in the 'burbs, her BFF gonna start working those curbs. What we call underage, pimps call early. How are you gonna compete? You're barely making ends meet. But this is where we come in, spitting the truth and then sneaking in the iPods. Wait for the change. In a time when crime is gloried in, as if killing our own kind could get you defiled. At least immortalized, in monuments made with graffiti – the highest honor the hood kid could receive. When the foundation is destroyed, the hearts of men are cold, and leaders are dropping like flies, look in my eyes. See the determination, muster up the bravery, and get tired of the sideline rush, the scrimmage line, homie. So help me.

18

DEAR BORED OF EDUCATION

Dear Board of Education, so are we. At no point in the lives we actually live do we sit in rows and listen to pontifications. At no point did Mama pass out written exams on how to wash the dishes. No. She pulled a stool up next to her at the sink, handed us a dishrag, and said, "Watch how Mommy does it. Now you try." Learning by doing – it's so crazy it works. Those stools felt like magical ladders into the grown-up world. Informational portals and wormholes into altered universes where kids were equals. Being made privy to info only those with driver's licenses and facial hair had. Who knew we were learning? No clue Pops was teaching time management and budgeting – Miniature Project Coordinators. He said, "I'm going to show you how to do these chores, and if they're done when I get home, then that allowance is yours. And maybe some ice cream." Remember when we were in kindergarten, and we learned about worms? Yeah, we went outside and played with worms. What a novel idea! Dear Board of Education, so are we. Dear Board of Education, all I've learned from your system is the fact that it's just a system that you set up.

If I just repeat what you just said in Jane Schaffer method then I pass, right? You're just testing my ability to regurgitate. If your best instructors are miserable, it probably isn't the kids' fault.
This pain I know firsthand. The grand learning moments. The innovative lesson plans that cause eyes to sparkle as if those students have caught rides on shooting stars. These lessons have wings, only to get clipped to fit in the low-res JPEG you call state standards. Why do you insist this is still the Industrial Age? My child is not a widget and school should not be an assembly line, making my daughter's diploma equivalent to an "inspected by 2235" stamp. Dear Board of Education, so are we. Dear Board of Education, there is not a Scantron on the planet that measures inspiration. This is what our teachers pass on that matters. But you'd rather them do the jig to the tune of AYP scores to avoid losing WASC right? NCLB has got us shucking and jiving, but you can't measure kids inviting their teacher to quinceañeras, soccer games, or waiting rooms at free clinics. I can name ten kids offhand who would still be in handcuffs if it wasn't for Mr Singer. Nick Luevano runs his own design firm yet failed the exit exam twice! Failed! Dear Board of Education, I mean, can we not google when the Magna Carta was signed? If your brightest stars are always dim, something's wrong with your glasses. If every place you touch on your body hurts, maybe your finger's broken. And the people who know a lot are not smart enough to know what they don't know? Did anyone ever suggest that we should test the test?

Dear Board of Education...My dear Board of Education, so are we.

END SCHOOL ZONE

MANERI 12/03 0318 PROPERTY CITY OF LOS ANGELES

19

RESPONSE FROM LECRAE

I wouldn't be the person I am today were it not for an emphasis on education and the power of God. My grandmother left home with today's equivalent of a 5th grade education. Her town didn't have the funding to keep the schools open. My mother grew up in one of the most impoverished communities in Houston, Texas. The education system was far below average. She taught me to read at 4 years old. She investigated programs around the city that would focus on my development. By 12, she made it mandatory for me to read the biographies of great historical leaders. Though she did her best, her efforts and my school system greatly contrasted. My father never made it past the 8th grade. Propaganda's "Dear Board of Education" reminds me of how hard my mother had to fight to break a vicious cycle that plagued my community. The words are reflective of our inefficient approach to education. I'm grateful for the expression and the exposure.

- Lecrae REACH RECORDS

20

THREE CORD BOND

And I watched them covet our style, our confidence, and our natural rhythm. Our terms of endearment, but not our struggle. And those products of the ghetto, what poverty can produce. And oddly enough, we giggled when you mimicked us. Sweet revenge. Homies not stupid can tell the difference between admiration and mockery, please. So we protected our music because truthfully, we thought it was all we had. And we watched y'all make a killing off of it, hip hop to jazz, Elvis to Fats Domino, Patra to Gwen Stefani. And the fact that those names are foreign is just what I'm pointing to. You imitated Jamaicans, attempted to grow dreads and commodified reggae – that's Marley's face on everything. Your children use faith as an excuse to smoke weed. So we grew angry, unaware of God's plan for rescue. But we don't know better. We've got a flawed version of personhood, identifying only by being victims of oppression. A true story. And I watched them covet your camaraderie, your sense of family, your food, and your work ethic, but not your struggle. And we were jealous. You had a homeland, a native tongue, and your parents spoke in it. We were just the offspring of the broken. Hopeless, so we all learned Swahili as if we knew we were from that region. Silly, we know, but what are you supposed to do when all you know is your closest cultural customs are similar to your captors? Huh, Pastor? It's easier to blame those economic woes on "filth" filtering through our borders, immigrant job hoarders. We should just deport them all on one bus. It's stupid us, broad-brush. We thought you were all Mexican, it's dumb, I know. I'm sorry, it's embarrassing, forgive us, we were jealous. We don't know better: selfish, angry, prideful. We'll even lynch and fight over the same piece of mud pie. Cómo se dice? Lo siento mucho. Por favor. We all need grace much more. That's a true story. And we coveted your privilege, your generational wealth, your unquestioned personhood, but not your struggle. And we felt it wasn't fair. We wanted your options, your grasp on proper doctrines and literature. It's silly, huh? Your American dream apple pie worked for you. So we worked for you. You made it seem so easy – grit your teeth, you could succeed too. We ain't know your story. Shoot, we thought white was white. Not Irish or Celtic or the Bolshevik plight.

Or the pain of bearing stains inherited. You said you weren't there, it ain't fair. You wouldn't dare, but we don't care. But we don't know better, you told us you struggle too – rednecks and trailer parks, me and you are cool. I hurt like you. But that was fire for the fuel that boiled into them riots. Y'all were so confused and truthfully, so were we. But now we understand that we suffered the same stain. We gain from a shared ancestor. We all descend from Adam's sin, riddles every inch of us, but now we see clearly that the Crimson Cord is one rope made from many strands. And each its own color, but now it clearly stands, dyed the color red from our Savior's blood shed. And a rope finds its strength from multiple lines wrapped around each other until they're all perfectly intertwined. So let's just call it even and walk through life knowing that a three cord bond is not easily broken.

21

RESPONSE BY BJ THOMPSON

When I first heard "Three Cord Bond," I was taken aback by the introspective look at our cross-cultural connections. For many of us, any conversation about race brings to the surface ugly feelings about things we'd rather bury or keep concealed. As a black American, one of the most stinging lines is about cultural appropriation: "Homies not stupid can tell the difference between admiration and mockery, please." Their perceived/real feelings of minority culture are being mocked and marketed by majority culture. It's saddening to see your sacred ethnic expressions talked about as a sign of dysfunction when used by minority groups, but a sign of status when stolen by majority culture. Cultural appropriation isn't the only feeling that rises as we connect cross-culturally, so does envy. "And we were jealous you had a homeland, a native tongue." False assumptions. "We ain't know your story. Shoot, we thought white was white. Not Irish or Celtic, or the Bolshevik plight. Or the pain of bearing stains inherited." Stereotypes. "And our immigrant job hoarders. We should all just deport them all on one bus." What is Prop saying? With all of these feeling and assumptions where does Prop point us to as the place of hurt and healing? Adam and Christ. In all Adam all distorted what was good but in Christ, all are able to be united, no matter their baggage.

- BJ Thompson BUILD A BETTER US

22

STRETCH-MARKS

If I could, I'd frame your stretch marks. You only get them two ways: By giving birth or dropping weight. Either way, serious pain. She is my pride. My bride. But before her, vato, my pride was my bride. Picture of endurance gave birth to our miracle. Those lines are memorials, freedom from the torture. Those pounds you put on were a defense mechanism. Like, "Maybe if I was ugly, then he would stop touching me." You endured the teasing of a fat girl on the track team but you kept running. You tuned out the ridicule and every calorie burned was cause for celebration. Those lines are victory laps, eternal gold medals. When I see them, they remind me of freedom. I'm so proud of you. How could I ever question your strength or ever doubt you? Your struggle inspires physical literature – the pain that gave life and the scars to prove it. If I could, I'd frame them.

23

WARM WORDS

Sometimes it's senseless. Sometimes it's a witness. The streets and the classroom can beat you senseless. Sometimes those paid to enforce the rules don't play by them. We stay violent. That's how it goes. On a cold day with headphones enjoying some Coldplay, reflect on the happenings, let's see what the Lord say. Inquire 'bout slots in heaven next to Trayvon, Oscar, and Emmett. Lord, I'm just curious – I don't know if they're in it. I know how their lives ended. It's got me seeking repentance for my desire for vengeance. That's why I pound these mics. Before the po-po takes another young life, they can be assured that their salvation's secure. Write for the confused, accused, abused, battered, and bruised. Two by two senators, treat us like citizens. I write to encourage an exodus. Yes, we are still slaves. Every time you pop your collar they giggle because you're still pickin' cotton. I write to outright outwrite you. Live outright righteous, right out your front door and write to explore, the right to explore because people need more. I might just ignore your plans for war and bless the amendments, despite my pigment. Never claim ignorance. Intent is intense. My Grandpop on Mom's side lived in tents – an outright Indian, a king among men. We are torn rip cords y'all can't afford to ignore it. Cracks in the shingles before the storm pours in, swore in soul ink on the grave of ancestors. Rep that name, Ancient of Days, and change that game. Spit that, in fact, grip that microphone with truth. In the midst of the twists and turns and scars and burns, I ain't the looking back type. Buckle up and hold tight. Oh this roller coaster, open eyes – both hands up – called life. Can't get enough of it, loving it. Although cold nights are more like slumber parties on Neptune, we are not left alone, held by faith alone. That's a no-brainer, 5 Sola soldier, usher in a legion of selfless rhyme-throwers on a cold night.

24

PRECIOUS PURITANS

If you would allow me a second to deal with some in-house issues, Pastor, it's hard for me when you quote the Puritans. Oh, the precious Puritans. Have you not noticed our facial expressions? One of bewilderment and heartbreak. Not you too, Pastor. You know, they were the chaplains on slave ships. Would you quote Columbus to Cherokees? Would you quote Cortez to Aztecs, even if his theology was good? It just sings of your blind privilege, wouldn't you agree? Your precious Puritans. They looked my onyx and bronze-skinned forefathers in their face, their polytheistic, God-hating face. Shackled, diseased, imprisoned face. And taught a gospel that says God had multiple images in mind when He created us in it. Their foredestined salvation contains a contentment in the stage they were given, which is to be owned by your forefathers superior, image-bearing face. Says your precious Puritans. And my anger towards this teaching screams of an immature doctrine and a misunderstanding of the gospel. I should be content, right? Isn't that what Paul taught, according to your precious Puritans? You get it but you don't get it. Oh, that we can go back to the America we once were, founded on Christian values. They don't build preachers like they used to. The richness of their revelations, it must be nice to not have to think or consider race. It must have been nice to have the time to contemplate the stars. Pastor, your colorless rhetoric is a cop out. You see my skin, and I see yours. And they are beautiful, fearfully, and wonderfully, divinely designed. Uniqueness. Shouldn't we celebrate it rather that act like it ain't there? I get it. Puritans got it. But how come the things the Holy Spirit showed them in the Valley of Vision didn't compel them to knock on their neighbor's door and tell them they can't own people? Your precious Puritans were not perfect. You romanticize them like they were inerrant. As if the skeletons in their closet are pardoned due to their hard work and tobacco growth. As if the abolitionists weren't racist and just pro-union. As if God only spoke to white boys with epic beards. You know, Jesus didn't really look like the paintings. That was just Michelangelo's boyfriend. Your precious Puritans. They got it but they didn't get it. There's not one generation of believers who figured out the marriage of proper doctrine and action. Don't pedestal these people. Your precious Puritans' partners purchased persons. Why would you quote them? Step away. Think of the congregation that quotes you. Are you inerrant? Trust me, I know the feeling. It's the same feeling I get when people quote me. If you only knew! I get it. But I don't get it. Ask my wife. It bothers me when you quote Puritans, honestly, for the same reason it bothers me when people quote me. Their precious Propaganda. I guess God does use crooked sticks to make straight lines. Just like your precious Puritans.

25

RESPONSE BY ERIC TURBEDSKY

This poem probably isn't about you. I'm a white pastor in a white town with a beard who reads Puritans. And it wasn't even about me — at least not initially. You see, I don't care what color you are or where you came from or the language you speak. I care about you knowing the most important man who has ever lived. Jesus.

The first time I heard this poem, I thought: "You go, Propaganda. Tell 'em like it is." I didn't get it. Like it is that complicated. I do have a tendency to turn men into heroes. To speak as if they are larger than life. I quote them, wear the jersey, and in some ways try to convince others that I'm with them. And so you should listen to me. But maybe my heroes are your villains. I also have a tendency to assume that my pursuit of the truth translates into my life. As if my morality is transformed by my study, and it is. Yet honestly, my heart has yet to catch up with my library. Why would you listen to me? I'm just another crooked man. See how complicated this gets? I'm a pastor. I'm supposed to be drawing straight lines. This is where the poem gets personal.

I preach a message that follows the story of how God is saving the world one broken, messed up man or woman at a time. Crooked doesn't even begin to explain the situation. I don't preach Puritans — I preach Christ — yet sometimes it sounds like I preach Puritans. Or worse, I preach me. And still God saves. Prop's message is plain. Use your words to serve people. Not everything you could say is helpful. That clever quotation might not be necessary. Consider history, ethnicity, language, and their relationship with you. Every conversation is a collision of private worlds, and some of them with deep roots that go back into an ugly past. But that's not all. Take it from one crooked man to another, I have seen God use people like us to draw straight lines. And it makes me twitch every time they mention my name.

- Eric Turbedsky
www.sovgraceoc.org

The goal was never saying no, but that my yes's count.

26

FORGIVE ME FOR ASKING

Question: this is embarrassing. Have you ever been scared you had no idea what you were talkin' about? Me too. Honestly perplexed, and I've lied. And so have you, Christians, lying! Like you've never had questions. Like you've never had a moment where your inner dialogue was all of the sudden in third person like, "You really buyin' all this?" Lying, like your eyes are 100% always satisfied by your spouse and you don't need accountability! Neither of which is biblical, by the way. Your eyes are never satisfied. Us, overgrown primates with egos. You're lying. You quote the devil when you declare yourself okay! You get it but you don't get it. Like you never planted your Chuck Taylors firmly on sinking sand. You're lying. We for centuries sing hymns to grace, this is why it's amazing. If it's not, then you don't understand, or you're lying. Which is why your friends don't believe you. There's as much of Jesus's blood on your hands as there is His. Are you sure you understand the cross? Muslim, excuse my boldness, but I think you're lying too. You don't have questions either? As if you never wondered why Allah's ears only hear directionally, and if you accidentally pointed slightly northeasterly you've blasphemed? As if the thought hasn't crossed your mind that Jihadists interpret the Quran correctly and you are what we Christians would call lukewarm. Which makes me much more like you than my Evan-jellyfish Church-ianity would allow me to admit. And you can call me on it. I'll deny it, just don't believe me. Because I'm lying. I strain at gnats – I focus on silliness. I act like God has joined a political party, just like you. As if you never thought, "What if I'm paralyzed and can't make my pilgrimage to Mecca, yet I follow the text better than all my family? Is there enough mercy for me?" I'm not gonna front like I understand your theology as well as I think I understand mine. But I know we agree on this: something is deathly wrong with us. And you, smarty pants. Don't front. Like of all that you don't know about the universe, you ready to draw a conclusion 'bout its origins? Maybe we don't know as much as we think we do. Science still can't explain yawning. Like you've never taken your worldview to its further conclusions – that if human behavior is just what protoplasm does at this temperature, there is no need for humanitarian effort. Because these atrocities aren't wrong; it's the universe just weeding out bad genes. Them is fingernails-on-chalkboard words, ain't they? You're lying. Maybe I'm wrong and you're right. We will find out the day after the world ends, won't we? Yeah, I guess we are all inconsistent. So can we just show each other some grace? You ever bury yourself in silent self-righteous guilt? Are there fresh tally marks on the walls of your brain prison, hoping that the count of good deeds outnumber the bad ones? Are your miserable failures your pride's badge of honor? When you count those tallies and the day the good outnumber the bad, pat yourself on the back. You have joined the rest of humanity. You too are lying. Like you've never thought, "Someone might catch me in my contradiction." Yeah, me too. You ever thought to yourself, "You have no idea what you're talkin' about"? Me too. Please forgive me for asking.

27

THEY REALLY NOT SO DIFFERENT

They really not so different. We all got issues – some are just more easy to identify. This one keeps tally marks, that one has lost count. This one has never thought twice, the type that loves rubrics. Just tell me how to do this. Practice makes perfect. That one questions everything, doesn't do too well with authority. Experience is the best teacher. Let me try my own hands. This one's got it covered, that one don't need a covering. This one's good visibly, that one failed miserably. This one got it all figured out, but so does that one, this one knows he's better than that one. That one's filth fills his nostrils – you stink of lawlessness, rebellion, frivolous and arrogant. That one knows this one's brainwashed, a drone who can't think on his own, who's prone to conform. You stink of vain repetition, judgement, arrogance. We've all got beliefs.

This one loves mirrors. He spends hours there perfecting his reflection, knowing full well it's lying to him. He just knows his religious cosmetics covers up his blemishes: feeding the poor, loving your neighbor, being tolerant. That's God's airbrush, right? That one hates mirrors, embarrassed of his reflection. He just knows if he blows enough, he'll be too high to notice it. Or even care, or question if it even matters. Like why buy into a system that feeds a man's ego, right? They really not so different. They both liars. Just that one's tired of doing it, this one thinks he's earned it, and that one don't deserve it. But that one agrees and begs for help like, "If I ask nicely, repeat this prayer, master these 12 steps, and clean up, then maybe I'll be redeemed." And this one agrees that if that one just "becomes more like me" that would be well. Both of you believe in your own means. This one is heaping up good deeds. He's involved in social justice. Let me prove he ever let a tool click but been so judgmental on souls you've left busies, As if his filthy rag righteousness is any less dirty than that one's. Homie, let's say they were gonna swim to Hawaii. That one made it one mile, this one made it 10. Neither one of them made it. Y'all are equally dead. That one tries to make it right but he's just heaping up Hail Marys. Like, "If I say I'm sorry, I'll be worthy of mercy." The foot of the cross has an even ground.

28

JESUS WASN'T A COMMUTER

Answer to the culture. Well, what is culture? We seem to have come up with answers and solutions. One, culture is this invisible monster that comes through the TV, internet, and schoolteachers and steals your kids. Hide yo' kids, hide yo' wife – they comin' for everybody. Let's get our Beauty and the Beast on, grab our biblical pitchforks, run into Hollyweird, and get the stomping! The other is more of a colonial approach. Those poor lil' colored kids don't know no better, living in these awful cities. Let's set those savages free and teach them to put down their desire for drugs, self-hate, and destructive behavior. Trade it for greed, financial dependence, and intellectual arrogance to assert over the other savages you colonizers haven't reached yet. Let me say it better: I've become fluent in that S.E.S. They call it gentrification. But in all your getting, get, and understanding, you don't get it, do you? You can fill your brain with a lifetime's worth of information and know nothing. You can know nothing and have a heart that breaks for a dying world – therefore not having anything to offer them. See, that's the problem. Them. There's no them. "Them" is us.

You are the culture. The city is you. Our Savior wasn't a commuter. He moved in to my city, can speak immigrant. The language of the broken, like the system and their English. I can read graffiti – Google Maps of the hood, my city. I'm a citizen and partaker of the culture and the problem, just like you. The ingredients are interchangeable. I know you get this. That's why you're here. You understand what the presence of a spraycan did to my self confidence. Listen, we livin' just enough for the city. Where I'm from, you either bang, slang, run or get increasingly efficient at putting the ball in the hole. Me? I stood under the light-pole, ciphering 'til morning. Come defending your name, crew, faith, and worldview. No curfew. We call it battling.
Y'all could film blogs on the validity of multisite churches and whether or not video feeds are biblical. That's a first world issue affecting one percent of y'all. Meanwhile, we're canceling quinceaneras 'cause lil mama finna be one.
We ain't got free wifi and I ain't got time to worry 'bout protected web keys. My son idolizes pimps – help me, megachurch pastor! There's the elephant in the room. You don't get it, do you? This is where culture is made. Every artist, politician, professor, and kindergarten teacher. Every convo you have at the grocery store. It's us. We are the culture. We are the city. We are the slaves. We are the problem. How could we possibly be the solution? We need someone from the outside to move in. The Savior moved in. Walked the same streets of your soul. See, the city is you. Now you move into the city. Walk the same streets I came from. And pray He comes. It prospers. Because if it prospers, you will too.

And suffering ain't suffering the second it finds meaning.

29

THE HEALTHY DON'T NEED DOCTORS

Once I heard this Middle Eastern carpenter say, "You know, the healthy don't need doctors."
It was such a curious phrase to me. Like, is he referring to gluttony? Like, what do you really want from me? And does it apply across the board, like the wealthy don't need money? Or the brilliant don't need book? And food is for the hungry? Or should I look around at my stuffed-to-the-brim drawers and closets. At that shirt or pair of pants I don't necessarily like but one day may decide I like so I might wear it. I would normally think to myself, "I need a bigger closet." Or look in my fridge at the day before yesterday's leftovers and think to myself, "Man, I'm starving, and we don't have anything to eat." Or maybe bemoan the cost of healthcare like, "How dare they charge that much per month!" Like, those doctors and pharmaceutical salesmen make millions – how dare they be available only Tuesday at 5. That's during rush hour traffic. I mean, what am I paying for? I wonder if you're like me. If you've ever attempted to dehumanize issues into budget line items or tax write-offs. Or better yet, pats on your own self-righteous backs, gathering these tally marks, as if God is somehow more happy with me when I round up and drop my change into that lil' box at the cash register. Or maybe a missionary came to your church and he talked about "the proverbial them." And as you wonder why there's no free wifi, you scrounge for a buck or two, give to your kids to put in the basket. It's a good lesson for them. Now can we move on and hear the message? After all, the gospel needs to be preached. And someone's got to pay for these lights on that stage. This carpenter's apprentice once said while he was locked up that he's "learned to be content in all stages." Whether his spirit wallet and bank account was on choking. Or swollen shrek pockets, he's good. I think I've got it on the broke side. Yeah, our contentment is in our Savior. Yeah, me and Him talk a lot during those times. But when those dollars are coming in, and those drawers are stuffed with clothes, and my cubbard got plenty of food...I just don't like that food, and fresh water flows from multiple rooms in my home. I wonder how silly I must look to the rest of the planet. Like I'm swimming in the ocean, praying for rain. I don't think we know how to abound. He said the healthy don't need doctors. It got me to thinking – am I healthy? I think Imma go clean out my closet. I don't need all this stuff.

30

I AM BECOMING...RESOLVED

"Be who you is, because who you ain't, ain't who you is." My mom's biggest desire was that I would be God's man and a man of God. That my desires would align with His. I can't say for certain if that dream of hers came true, but I do know this: I'm determined to be who I am made to be, not what anybody else is made to be.

31

RESOLVED

So what are they going to say about us, huh? Early 21st century humanity, when history tells the truth: America on the brink of war with 3 countries consecutively. And the church? Well, one part was making reality shows about decadence. And the other? Well, they wrote blogs about how the other part was wrong. And the rest? Well, they didn't have running water or the governmental right to practice their faith, so they just died off. They say our nation is on its way to hell as if it's ever been in heaven in the first place. It's time to redeem the time.

32

CONQUER

We all know the moment well. You hear it in your hunger. Your feet turn to tree trunks. I won't be moved. And the conquerer inside exhales a war cry. He sings. Shoulder blades expand into wings. Not fearless. See, that's a clear indication of ignorance. You ain't done your homework, brought a switchblade to a gunfight. No, it's in the face of resistance. It's when it pales in comparison. The promise of the possibility far surpasses the perils of the pursuit. We persevere. That Plains Indian bison hunter gets the biting at your backbone. You can taste the adrenaline. Please, let your boys watch Man vs. Wild. There's a Bear Grylls in all of us, caged in our cubicles and smartphones. We conquer! 16th century Pilgrims braving the toughest winter this land has ever seen – 4 in 6 settlers die that winter. Conquer. Teachable. Let the natives show you how to harvest crops from beach sand. It seems like the planet is fighting back. Conquer. Daniel in the belly of the beast – capital of Babylon – refused to eat like a king. I don't need your love, I'll take my chances at a slumber party with lions before I'll sell out. Conquer. D-Day, storming Normandy shores. The bloodiest war this world has ever seen but democracy is worth it. Conquer. Slave trade, our grandmothers were sold off auction blocks. They checked her teeth like she was cattle or a race horse. Billy clubs, fire hydrants, wild dogs. Lynchings, Jim Crow laws, assassinations. None of it matters, we march. Refuse to let my grandkids drink from a separate fountain. Two by two sit-ins – we desire service. Nervous but we deserve to be treated like citizens. Conquer. Let's take it home. Conquer! Look them OGs in their faces! Jump me, chase me home, threaten my lil' brother, but I am not joining your set. I'm not slanging for you. I am not nor ever will be a statistic. I ain't going to jail for none of y'all. Conquer! You guard your heart, starve your eyes. Turn off the porn. There's a God look-alike queen counting on your patience. Courage. The guts to say no and to keep your hands off another man's blessing. Fight! Don't punk out. You'll be a slave to your sex drive. Murder your flesh. Conquer. I will clean toilets, mop floors, shine shoes, ask you if you'd like fries with your order, clean up dog droppings. I will wash windshields at the stoplight before I'll let my family go hungry. Men work! No shortcuts, no cheating. Night job, night school, night shift, night train, I'll walk home in the rain. No pain, no gain. The honor of an honest day's pay. Tucking my little girl in with pride. Building her dreams with my bare hands. Every nail, every screw in this house I can trace to each of Daddy's gray hairs and wrinkles. Conquer. You got the same 24 hours I got. You got the courage to not waste yours? 4th quarter. Down by 1. Championship. 3 seconds left. Free throw line. No fouls to give. You take courage or ride the bench. There is no other alternative. Conquer! You'd better find it! Courage. Man up.

33

RESPONSE BY REV. LEONCE B. CRUMP JR.

What is manhood? Is it brutishness? Can it be reduced to virility? Power? No, not necessarily. We were not all made physically imposing. We were not all etched out of stone. But all men know that endurance is the enduring characteristic of a man. Add responsibility. Chivalry. Leadership. These don't require imposing size or dazzling intellect. They simply require that you accept your place in the world as a man. Yes, it's okay to be that. To be manly. To be masculine. To reenter the calling that was placed on him, the one who failed, who followed, who fell. Adam let us down, and in the face of the fall being a man has become increasingly difficult. These thoughts are what Prop's words invoked in me. It seems in the wake of postmodernity that we've lost sight of what it means to be a man. The postmodern man is unsure and unsettled. Willing to live in a basement rather than work to earn a place. Content, in a social-emotional sense, to eat road kill rather than hunt. It's disheartening. It's shameful. And because of the present state of things, it sometimes feels villainous to be a man. Watch any network television show with a father, and you will find a bumbling idiot. Movies often relegate men to the same role. Clueless. Aloof. Emasculated. And then there is this powerful poetic work, a call to conquer, to man up, to tap into how we were made. Men were made to lead – sacrificially, boldly. Men were made to protect, to provide, to be both tender in heart and strong in will. These are the categories that arise in me as I savor this work. Oh, there is a strong push against this "traditional" definition of manhood, but who defines the terms? Culture? No. He who made, makes the categories, boundaries, and beliefs by which we live. Only God can define man. He has. He is the One who made the first man, and put inside of him His Spirit. The One who gave him a calling, work to do, and then a wife. The One who, no matter how much one may suppress it, put a longing inside us, men, to be more. To reflect His image. To display His glory, not distort it. This. Is. Manhood. Don't shrink back. I can't shrink back. Not in the face of the call to conquer!

- *Rev. Léonce B. Crump Jr.*
RENOVATION CHURCH ATLANTA

Creators not consumers.

34

I STILL DON'T SEE IT

It took us so long to get here. And here really ain't that special. Was it all worth it? Was it all you hoped and wished for? I remember the daydreams of a preteen boy on Grandma's porch. A motley crew of ashy-kneed colored boys yelling, "That's my car!" when nice ones rolled by. Bathing in that summer afternoon sunset. Heads flat on the concrete, eyes straight into the sky, as to drown out the smog and drug transactions we were obviously surrounded by. One day I'm going to make it. But what is "it"? Objects? Things? All to realize that calm really ain't that calm. And the struggle is much more enjoyable when the end ain't clutched. Like the moment you realize you're consumed with first world problems. I guess that means you made it. Face it. It's eerie how uncomfortable it is when we get too comfortable. It's kind of like the notion that if you accept this set of notions then your soul's okay. And you're searching for new mountains to climb as if you conquered the first one. You ain't done. You're just comfy. Is this what we've been working towards? The journey to okayness, life with equilibrium, homeostasis? Hope you don't mistake it for peace. It feels like your tenacity has been moved to the suburbs. And perfect lawns and neatly aligned trees and safe parks. A school's a good place to raise a beer belly, right? Identical strip malls on every corner of your mind can feel a little claustrophobic. And it's there that you realize there is no "there" because this kind of perfect just ain't working. Don't you dare close them curtains. It ain't nighttime. And you don't need another object. And that is not beauty. It's eerie how uncomfortable it is when we we get too comfortable. And when they're closing all the curtains to convince you that it's nighttime, don't believe them. Don't believe them. And when they tell you, "It's a must-have and you can't live without it," listen, you don't need it. You don't need it. And when they tell you, "Sweetie, this and only this is beautiful," tell them, "I don't see it."

35

JPEG

The moment is so awkward. I ain't know who should talk first. I don't know what to tell you. I don't know what I call it, except clear. Resolute. You. The image is so rich with irony. Clones in front of their audiences yellin' stop me if you heard this one. The quintessential hipster. At least he's a good listener. Pardon the pun, it wasn't intended. So cool in their TOMS shoes. So cool. He raises his hands as to halfway clap, as to halfway approve. If only you stuck to rap. If only you stuck to poetry. If only you had an only. You're the whitest son of a Panther I know. It's hip hop but not what you think. You think I think I'm Mexican. The image is blurry, ain't it? Y'all remain clueless. I battle my alarm and wage war with my to-do list. The egregious amount of hands I got on the little bit of time I've got that ain't even mine in the first place. Don't include me in sacred and secular debates. It's old and I don't care what you call yourself. My Google Map has never changed. Same red pin I'm aimed at. That's a low-res issue, like I don't know what to tell you. It's a goulash, hand-picked mosaic. All are key ingredients, 139 type. The cat that got my tongue has been holdin' on for dear life for so long. No Grammys or Stellars, just bars that come from under the cellar and soar higher than cellular. Let's network. I can't tell you my net worth. I've honestly got no clue. My Journey told me ends were never fuel for choosing the type of tool we usin'. That would be so low resolution.

36

NEED YOU MORE THAN EVER

One part of me hates you. Another part is jealous. A small part of me thanks you. Your negligence has given me a reason to breathe. A stepfather, raising a worthless man's daughter. If you've ever seen her smile, you wouldn't question why I bother. It's my cross to bear. A come-off-the-bench dad, JV second string, substitute stepdad. Listen, I understand some things just don't work out. Her mom can be a handful, believe me, I know. But that's not your daughter's fault. Oh! We got the gifts you bought, but she would trade them all for a half hour of your time. Me and her have bonded. It's been years. She calls me Daddy now. You don't know how long I've yearned to hear that word you ain't worthy of. She see you as a stranger. She's scared of your touch, yet her lil' brain's conflicted. She misses you and don't know why. It's crazy – sometimes I see my sister's personality in her, so tempted to say she gets her eyes and sense of humor from me. I know that's delusional. But I am so afraid of losing her, falling into the you-shaped black hole in her 6-year-old soul. It cuts my tongue but she needs you more than ever. That's how much she means to me. I'm willing to admit she does need you. I bleed for my lil' girl. Her very breath is a blessing, from doing her laundry to tryin' to explain sovereignty. I will love her as my own, be the father God called me to be. Yet honesty compels me. My dude, she needs you.

37

REDEFINE CUTTER

73rd and San Pedro. Uncle Sunny and Odell. Take your pick on what kills you: bullets, cancer, or jail. What a life. I came out of a town of gangs, and a gang of grace, 'cause fo' sho' sin abounds. 'Round these parts, crowns are made of tin foil, and these boys play Halo with real guns, lay low. Right there, I fling swing that twice-born rhetoric. Family. Our Papi pound the ground and out came all humanity. Write heavy-handed Sharpie ink laced with mercury. Write raps that are magnetic, drawing out impurities. 'Round the time the good Lord took Mamma Winnie, the light bulb turned on – this world ain't my home. I huddled up to Triage with curb servers and griots. That's such a LA reference – it's cool if you ain't get it. For those who would listen, I'll break you out of your radio prison and redefine blackness, manhood, and time. Shape and define culture, let me fashion you some shades, introduce you to a new trend that transcends the will of men. Good Lord. I ain't a product.

I ain't apologizing. You ain't a number. Pay them no mind. Ring the alarm, Prop redefines cutter, carving truth in his heart and love on her arms. Literate in graffiti, I am not at all kidding. I'm from the heart of the city that Stevie lived just enough for. Jackson, Mississippi: my people toiled the soil and sharecroppers popped coppers and seen their kin lynched in. That was the lynchpin of mass migration into Texas, rest of us pushed west still. Manifest Destiny of a black American family – wanted better for their kids and landed in Southern Cali. Who knew it was a war zone my uncles got recruited in. Cousin Sean and Qiana seen death out in Compton. And they ain't fallen victim, cousin Brandon either. We should have framed the tax return that got us to Covina! There I met a mic and spraycan instead of blue rags, fell in love with flares y entiendo Spanglish. Stand on my own two and rep the Son of Man. Branded my own chest so I could never blend in.

38

SINEMA

Finding further frustrations in the fact that my flesh problems ain't fixed in 25 minutes or less. Yes, it's so far from sitcoms where Mom is so silly and Dad is so stupid. And every major life lesson ends wit' hugs and laugh tracks. And precocious lil' sisters hit you with a zinger. No, no Zack & Cody, hey Jessie, Good Luck Charlie, and sometimes Cory don't get Topanga. This boy met the world and loved it a lil' too much. I was Breaking Bad wit' Theory, Big Bangin' wit' Mad Men. When the season ended, my House of Cards came crashing. All the desires of my heart led to The Walking Dead. Dang. This really ain't a sprint, is it? Some of us get lost and come crashing on jagged shores. No neat little bow. Everyday we pitch our tent one day closer to eternity. Whether storms of life or aimless drifting in hopeless oceans, the anchor of my soul is the same light on the shore, my peace in the troubled sea. I found my true North. The reason for all songs. The light beam that pierces the fiercest of London fog.

39

YOU GOTTA DIG

Find it somewhere in your soul, the last bit of strength that will take you on home. Find it somewhere in your heart, to put the past in the past and go back to the start. Selfish, prideful, come get an eyeful. An ugly dark stain on a once wonderful resume. Leisurely strolls down the road of perdition, leaves a man wishing for his old position. I know it's so tempting, but it's still so empty and if I ever lose sight, come and get me. You gotta dig. She's a jewel in your crown. Don't trade a million dollar future for a nickel right now. Mama said leave a place better than you found it. And looking in your eyes, I realize how profound that is. Dig like there's no tomorrow. Dig like you're living on time that's borrowed. Dig, homie, it's in there somewhere. Dig like your life depends on it, because it does! And Grandmama touched down, fresh from Dallas, Texas – a block from Ghost Town. Natural born rider, Watts Riot survivor. Loved her four kids but them streets were a beast. And by God's grace alone, three out of the four made it. Now the son of second born is rocking microphones. It is so lovely. I wish it could hug me. It's dirty and it stinks but it's mine for the keeps. Me, the son of a "9-to-5'er" civil rights and Vietnam War survivor. They told my Grandpappy that blacks were not human, but that didn't stop the movement. You gotta dig! Find it – when the wind sings the songs of the dedicated few who wouldn't fall headlong and find it. Watch me tighten my belt when the prayers of this rapper are a desperate cry for help. I desire a higher outcome than weed, get you. Forgive me if I dismiss you – it's not to diss you. I am not a Rasta, don't let the dreads fool you, although I take Jah serious. It's cool, let me school you, dig? I can't say I'm not tired or never felt a little envious of names on flyers. Empty-handed and homesick, although I know my flow's sick. If y'all only knew how cold this road gets, you'd dig. If I ever lose sight, come and get me. You gotta dig! I'm not the artist – I'm the canvas. Remind me of my own words even though I can't stand it. Hold me accountable, call me on my laziness, call me by my birth name, look me in the face, and dig. If I ever lose sight, come and get me.

40

RESPONSE BY JAMIE TWORKOWSKI

"Dig" was the first poem I ever heard Prop do. I had heard his name but didn't know his stuff. We were up in Canada for a retreat, part of a group of 150 people at a beautiful spot on the Princess Louisa Inlet in British Columbia. There were a lot of successful people there, a lot of leader folks. It could be assumed this was a group of people who "have it all together." It was early in the trip when Prop was asked to share a poem. We were all still getting our feet wet, asking names and where do you live and what keeps you busy. Prop dove in. By the time he got to "put the past in the past," my eyes were full of tears. By "come and get me," I was crying. The whole thing seemed to say, "This is me. This is a little bit of my story. This is some of where I come from. This is some of what I struggle with." It changed the day and set the tone for the entire event. Prop's honesty gave everyone in the room permission to be honest, permission to be real and raw. We didn't need to fake it. We didn't need to have it all together. I remember the trip to Canada as one of my all-time favorites. The conversations were rich and I walked away with deep new friendships, Prop included. And when I look back, "Dig" was the turning point. "Dig" was the spark.

– Jamie Tworkowski
FOUNDER OF TO WRITE LOVE ON HER ARMS

41

HANDS OFF THE BRAKES

I have conveniently misplaced my parachute pack. I don't fear gravity. If you need me, come find me where the GPS can't – that's where I'm setting up camp. I followed the riverbend to fly fish in the future. Caught me marlin swimming in oblivion. Youthful curiosity. Why live if you ain't living? Save your kerosene – don't leave the light on for me. If all goes to plan, me and the fam ain't returning.

42

WHAT IF YOU KNEW?

Would you start a music career if you knew you would never grow past local? Maybe sell about 100 copies, and the most to ever come to a show is 15-20 folks? All your events are holes in the wall. But your best friend, who you started with and learned instruments with, would make it to super stardom. Wildly successful. And the entirety of your career existed solely as a diving board for that dude's unimaginable success. He will be platinum. And you? A platform. And you, local. Loyal. Would you still do it? Would you have quit your job, dropped out of school, and saved your allowance for that first piece of equipment? What if you never make it but all your friends do? Would you sacrifice your home life for a business if you know that it will never quite turn the corner but the lil' dude that swept the floor is on the cover of Forbes? Would you? Would you have even written a single paragraph for a book, opened the doors of a church, opened up that storefront, applied for 501c3, endured the audit, began online school? Sacrificed sleep and marriage, knowing it will never go any further than the 10 to 15 people you started with – 5 being your own kids. Would you have recorded one syllable – one? Knowing the only reason you were given this gift and passion is for someone else's platform? Would Mandela have uttered one word, knowing he'd lose his wife and children to nearly thirty years of prison? And small-minded people nitpick at his flaws after his death. Was the abolishment of apartheid worth it if he saw the future? Would you have even signed up for Little League, knowing you'd remain a high school legend, knowing you wouldn't even get to D3? But your lil' brother...Hall of fame. Hmm, would you do it, if you knew greatness would never come? Just struggle. The type of struggle that forges fortunes for lumps of coal...Would you do it? Me neither. Mystery is such a strange gift. The unknown is such a wonderful veggie. It's a good thing we can't see the future. Because we would ruin it every chance we get.

Don't change your life to create, just see the beauty of now.

43

I AM BECOMING...AND WILL ALWAYS BE

I think I've found the most peace in the concept that theology nerds call "the already, but not yet." Basically, it's the concept that believers in Jesus were already perfected and completely saved at the moment of salvation, but clearly the world still sucks royally and so do humans. As a matter of fact, I found that humans throughout time have continued as we always have. We are good and bad, brilliant and stupid. The same civilization that mapped the stars and built pyramids also sacrificed people to rain gods. And us, who put people on the moon and made cell phones, also populate Walmart. It's crazy. We will always be growing, but at the same time, we were made right already. But we ain't right just yet. I'm cool with being a lifelong learner.

44

I'M SO DONE WASTING WORDS

I'm so done wasting words. A not-so-vivid imagery. Enemy wages war and silly me is still scrimmaging. Radio prisoners still rape for ratings. I sorry I didn't get it. Like, the whole world is listening and that's the best you could come up with? An artistic obligation to defend beauty and truth. Rap repeating dumb behavior – that's a symptom of autism. A "micro" of the "macro." Welcome to the great cultural dumb down. I'm so done wasting words now. But who doesn't know this side? I'm about to "command Z" you. Un-bite the apple, no "control C" and "control V" you. Take these new raps from handclaps to finger snaps to grid. De-saturate how I live. Multiply my layers, drop the opacity, make it transparent.
I call it God's Photoshop. This here is a collection of the boldest stock photos. When the part of you that expects failure speaks too loud, download these images. Fake left and click right. Tell the road less traveled to buckle up and hold tight! This is rap and poetry, emceeing and imagery. Mic and the canvas, art ambidextrous.
I'm so through wasting words.

Often
I witness beauty
Lofty
My brain is puny
Perfect
Distribution
of excellent execution
and I'm in awe

45

AND NOW

And now, you oceans. You mighty blue tides. Tell me your stories. Spare no details and pull no punches. Your legacy. As curious as dark matter or the heart of a woman. Your sunsets. Show me no mercy. Tell us of how we failed you and made you proud in the same breath. How hands that lay waste to hopes and dreams can be the shapers of epic destinies. How every triumphant march is full of Achilles heels. How all our heroes are flawed and fallen. It's fun. It's fast. It's slow. It's frustrating. It's longsuffering. Patience-building. Smelly. Good. Bad. Beautiful. It's both and not either or. You bone gardens, remind me that I am animated dust. And so is the pedestal I put my mother on.
And the platform I stand on to reach your ears.
And sit in your hard drives.

46

PERFECT PICTURE

The perfect picture. The space and time splitter. The Augustan calendar plumb line. We all know what common era means, please. I'm telling you this is epic – wait for it, Imma fix it. The promised neck-crusher wit' a bruised heel. It's so real. The image the law was picturing. Prophets were tryin' to concoct words about breathing word. Get it? Breathing words about the Word that breathes breath of life and invented both. Whoa. Word. The great promise. Stay stuntin' like my daddy. The great I am, great I told you. The system flip over-er. The overture you missed. The back is the front. Left side up. The greater and higher jihad, the greater revolution. Earthly kingdoms are pitiful. Second in rank, equal in essence. Laughing at demigods. Them a fraud. But the joy set before him. The kingdom is backwards. Rulers serve the servant king, suffering servant. The endless and eternal. I owe you one, older brotha. The Savior – irrespective of race, rank, or gender. The good news incomparable. I'm all you've got, partna. The "Good luck without me, bub." The "It's all good, your smell don't bother me. I love you." Still sitting at the right hand, giggling at Earth's kings. Your entire empire's a card castle. No hassle. The sound that is person came and camped with underlings, who is the light and life of all human beings. The Emmanuel. The "yeah, I'm that guy. I'm that dude." The "I'm period." The second person fully God, King, Him. The "I'll take that and raise you one." The raised one. The owner of death's keys. The bondage-breaking and living and breathing liberty bell who never cracked. The warning, the dawn of the last morning. The "I'll be right back. Imma deal with this a lil' later. I am not at all shook in any way by Satan. Can a painting scare the painter or does it just destroy the canvas?! Until then, I'm waiting for these suckers to prop my feet on. And Pops says I'm on my way to scoop my bride up. Let's roll, girl." Lion, lamb. 1 of 3 in 1. The prophesied Messiah. Our prophet, priest, and king. Jesus. Yeshua.

You can do anything you want, just not everything you want.

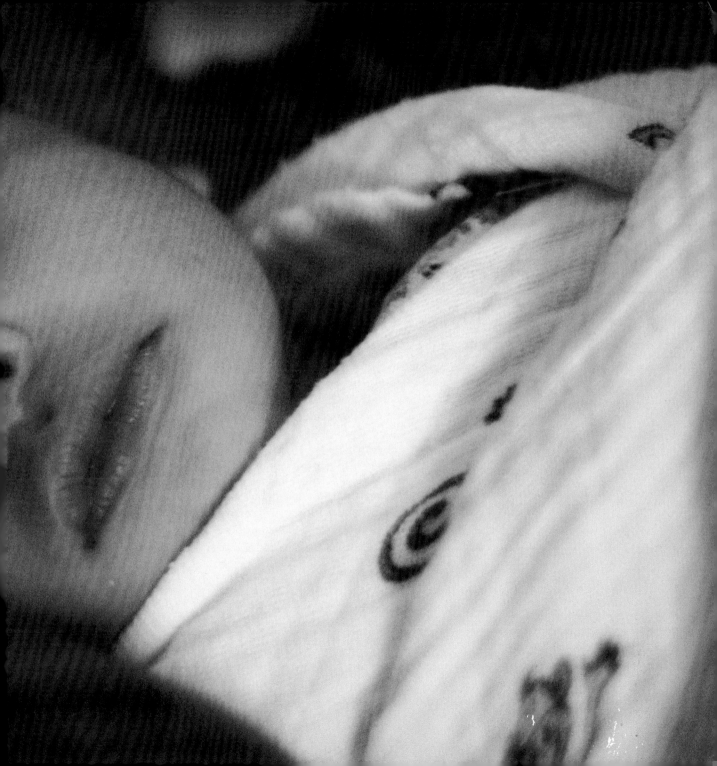

47

BE PRESENT

I tend to think of life in movie clips. Tweetable moments. Somehow I've convinced myself that they last longer that way. I was proven wrong when my wife called my phone my black wife. I thought it was funny – we giggled. Single men take notes. I'm no expert, but I don't think she was kidding. She went on but I don't remember most of the rest. I was too busy mentally composing a tweet where I quote her with some clever hashtag about marriage and how awesome my wife was to pay attention to her. I think what snapped me back was the silence that indicated that I was supposed to speak then. I told my dad that story to get some sympathy, something to bond over. My Dad, Vietnam veteran, hopelessly charming. On his 4th marriage. Dad. Rather than the traditional nod men give each other when they agree, he began to lay out a case as to why he failed as my mother's husband. He said it was the same reason half of his platoon in Vietnam died. Same reason you are deathly afraid of your daughter becoming a teenager. You can't hear anything past the explosions, either the one you remember or the one you anticipate. The former paralyzes. Living life in the rearview mirror, driving full speed across all six lanes into oncoming traffic. Or so shellshocked you're too stupid to duck when the bullets fly. Or the latter. So goal-oriented that your life is a game of capture the flag. So fixated on the finish line that you stepped right into a land mine. You're so ready to attack the day, frustrated because you can't find your keys. Too focused on the traffic you finna sit in and meetings you're about to miss to realize that you were holding them up the whole time. Slow down. You have been hypnotized by possibility. Son, I couldn't hear past the bombs. The first one didn't kill me and the next one didn't even happen. He told me a love story: She was born before me and knew me from before. And at the moment of conception and eternal connection. And although I didn't know it then, I'd fight for her affection. A war we've been waging from day one of creation. And only when you lose her do you learn to appreciate her, like even when I'm with her, I'm itching to get rid of her. I'm tryin' to learn my lessons, son, I swear to you I'm feeling her. I can never get enough of her and to this day I love her. She only gives you one shot. Blow it and she's gone. I took advantage of her. That's why I'm telling you this, You can't rush her or slow her down. Keep here on her side. She will slip through your fingers. Her name is Time. She told me a secret. Multitasking is a myth. You ain't doin' anything, just everything mediocre. She begged me to stop stretching her thin and stuffing her full, stop being so concerned with the old her and future her. But love her now. Her presence is God's present. You should be that; present. I guess I've been through a divorce. I'm no longer married to my phone. I'm ready to be here, now.

48

RESPONSE BY CAMERON STRANG

Next time you're at a restaurant, look around. Notice the families. The couples. The friends. Just watch them for a minute. Most of them are sitting there, together, silently. They're looking down at their phones, scanning, swiping…checking what else is out there. Probably looking at updates from people they barely know, while ignoring the people they're with. Propaganda's "Be Present" is completely right. We've become a society more connected to that thing in our pockets than the actual people in our lives. Multitasking is a myth. But Prop is lucky. I learned his lesson the hard way. A couple of years ago, I went through a divorce. Pressure from work, stress, finances, whatever—over time, it eroded our foundation, changed us, and eventually the marriage crumbled. By the time we realized it, it was too late. Looking back now, I realize that during the hardest seasons of the marriage, I was hurting but never dealt with it because I was filling those voids with distractions. My vice was work. My laptop became a coping mechanism, and it just made things worse. It's human nature to look for distractions and escapes when we're hurting. Some people drink to numb the pain. Some distract themselves from it with busyness. And when some people are feeling unloved, they look to their phones for validation. Addiction…coping…distraction. It's all cloth that comes from the same thread. For me, the main thing that's pushed me to be my better self is that I have a young son. Through all this, I know he's watching. That makes me live for something bigger than myself. It makes me pursue God more intently. And it makes me be intentional with so many aspects of my life that I didn't really think about before. After the divorce, I turned my life upside to focus on the things that truly matter. I took time off and have hard boundaries to protect a work/life balance. I got involved in church. And I make sure that every day my son and I are together, I don't waste a minute of it. Being intentional. Being present. That's all that matters now. I never want my son to grow up thinking that whatever is on the other end of that phone or that laptop is more important to me than him. So, if we're at a restaurant, I'll never have my phone out. I'm there, with him, talking, engaging—letting him know this moment, right now, with him, is that the only place I want to be. Have you ever been at a party talking to someone and the whole time they're glancing over your shoulder? It's like they're scanning the room actively looking for someone more interesting to talk to. It makes me want to walk away. How about this? I have a crazy idea. Ready? From now on, let's look people in the eye when we're talking to them. Let's quit scanning the room, or scanning our phones. Let's live in the moment. Let's quit being distracted. Let's focus on the stuff that really matters. Life is about real connection. Not a phone. Not a laptop. It's about being present—all in, 100 percent, no distractions. Trust me, Prop is right. I may have learned that the hard way, but it's a lesson that has changed me for the better.

- Cameron Strang
FOUNDER OF RELEVANT MAGAZINE

Crensh

EXIT ⬇

w Blvd

ONLY

49

ALPHA MALE

Awkward silent moment. I think we all know it well. Well, probably those who are most well-acquainted are you alpha males. See, I don't respond too well to alpha males. My father was one. I know that moment well. When your own mouth tells on you, making it painfully obvious that your self-assessment is fatally flawed. That's an awkward moment. Know-it-all little boys covered in facial hair and youthful arrogance. Is it possible you're not the smartest one in the room? Is it possible that the manufacturer knows a little more about their products than you do? That is why they wrote directions. We men never outgrew our toys. They're just much more expensive now. Wouldn't you much rather do something right than twice? This is awkward. You have proven what we all thought of you! I don't do too well with alpha males. If you're just stronger and louder than me, I'm supposed to listen. Your obnoxious Affliction shirt is the scepter of your kingdom. You are still just that 6th grade bully, oblivious to the fact that the lunch money you just stole belongs to your future boss. This is awkward. I don't do too well with alpha males, but my problem is in reverse. You ever disagree with someone just to pick at them? They might be right but you ain't wanna give them the satisfaction…This is awkward. I struggle with the concept of police and military. My father was a Vietnam and civil rights war vet, they had him almost die for a country that barely let him vote. You turned fire hydrants on little girls, water pressure ripped skin off. I'm supposed to submit. This is awkward. But is it possible that I don't get it? And my submission is to the King and not so much middle management. But if I truly love the King, I wouldn't fight against his leadership appointees. Maybe I don't know everything. And you, "oh yeah, can you beat me up?" Boys. If your only response to logic and reason is that or, "So? Shut up!" Maybe you shouldn't be in charge. Homie, beefing with the blue dot on your Google Map as if it's a personal attack on your intelligence to think you're lost? Listen. Scream all you want, no one's listening. You can't follow directions or a blue dot, so why should anyone follow you? Maybe in the same vein as Rosa Parks, the best way to stand is to sit and that's brilliant. If you can't follow, you can't ever lead. Real men recognize authority. Sometimes you've gotta bow down to man up.

50

BECAUSE

We don't assume we're at ease because the news cameras leave. Because closing curtains don't make stars disappear, and Band-Aids don't cure cancer, but they sure are comfort, and what's wrong with giving comfort? Because feelings fade and generosity is contagious. Because pain is not sexist or racist. We could learn a thing or two from the tenacity of tragedy. Once it locks onto your scent, it's just a matter of time and the only difference between mortgage and food banks is moments. Precious moments. Because objects rust and break, memories fade, but moments are eternal. We give moments. Because we've been given them. Because we live with the tension of how undeserving we are for the breath we have. Breaths, moments, are gifts, freely given. Who am I to hoard them? We give. Because we love and we love. Because we were loved first. Who am I to hoard it?

51

TOO CREATIVE

I was recently told I was too creative, not Christ-centered enough. And the peeps we tryin' to reach wouldn't understand your speech. I told them it's cool. It's not an issue. I ain't so judgmental. Thanks for the advice, I just ain't afraid of heights. Like Christ wasn't afraid to mix spit with mud. As if he couldn't fix vision with one word, I'm sorry. I get my creativity from my Father. Have you ever been to the aquarium? Google the coral reef, for Pete's sake. Thanks for the advice, but I'm not afraid of a blank canvas. Ain't afraid to be the canvas. I've been marred in the Potter's hand and God don't use erasers. Off on purpose. What keeps you up at night? Are you afraid of budget meetings? Or the board of directors? Thanks for the advice but I ain't afraid of gravity, since His majesty came and grabbed me. I've often wondered how loud an alarm clock needs to be to wake a dead man? Maybe you're right! I'm just too creative. See, I am afraid of being wrong but if I am, tell me. I ain't afraid of correction – humbly embrace lessons. You shouldn't be afraid of city permits. I'll submit to the process. There's not one city permit that can stop what Elohim permits. I'm so comfortable with sovereignty. So done wasting words and so tired of lying to the Father and the mirror. That's where I get my courage from. My spine isn't naturally stainless steel. You can get freely what I learned from failing miserably. I guess the question shook me because, honestly, I'm terrified. Terrified of wasting time. But you could bet your good graces I ain't afraid of their faces. Hearts of men wax cold, out-your-mind sold. It takes away freedom. Your life is not golden. It's the guts to say no, then nosedive. Follow commandments that don't make sense. God says learn to walk worthy. And if you understood the cross, you would see that command is such a paradox. I think I understand now, between heresies and Pharisees. Between schemes to get rich and work to attain wealth. This is why I graciously smile because truthfully, they're scared. Scared like most of us are. Scared that you've just wasted a weekend, spent a couple hundred bucks to do the same thing you've been doing. Scared you're all talk and that your ideas ain't original. You are just like your parents. And you are okay, mediocre. Your product is mediocre. And the best you've ever been is so-so. This ain't a movie, you might go bankrupt. A fail like the rest of us. Like, I'm scared that I'm irrelevant! Like, is this really happening? Am I still rapping – a grown man doin' the same thing I was doing at 15? And you're scared you only give as a tax write-off. Or, give to Africa to prove you ain't racist. When's the last time you brought the gardener a cup of water? I don't even know our groundskeeper's name, and that vato wears a name tag! You're scared, like I am, that these chairs are way comfortable. And the cost of that light could have fed Angola. And honestly, it don't bother me. Scared that we're born eagles, walking among chickens, as if these agitated shoulder blades never sprouted wings. I was once told I was too creative. And that shook me to the core. I have no excuse for fear. I should be rollerskating around Saturn, looking down at satellites. If you muster up the bravery, you'll get this one day, that we fooled you. This ain't a conference, this is a runway. Why ain't you flying?

Me? I'm just shaping the convos that will occur after my burial.

52

TELL ME YOURS

I'm honestly not looking for "thank you's" because I don't deserve them. I didn't earn them. But you can thank South Central, the San Gabriel Valley. Run up PCH to East Bay and thank Lake Merritt. Every TurfWalker and scraper bike. When ya see one, say thanks for Prop's music. Poseidon who made sure the bar was high in the cypher. Krystal, Kevin, Corey, the other black family in Valinda. Thomas Polkinghorn. He's why I even liked rap. Thank the I.E., Foundation. The hardest battles I've ever been in against Triune, Dead-Eye or Ishues. Breuman, Zaragosa, Wilbur family introduced me to the gospel. Reynosa, Coleman, Whitenhill, Robles tribe, My Sri Lankan twin Holden. Ronnie David Robles. He's first to put a spraycan in my hand and imagination expands, why my art is ambidextrous. I owe you one, hermano! Trujillo, Montez, Sales, Carrasco. Told you I grew up with the vatos! Leon, Myron, Junie, Mrs. Venita Shells, Uncle Ray, Aunt Fannie Mae, Vakaa Rose, and Aunt Ethell. Mr. Jeffery, Mrs. Cronan, Mr. Paliki came to get me when I was ditching U.S. History, trying to keep up with Trevor Penick. Thank David Utley. He told me he thought God made black people by smearing them with feces. And Brad Sutton, who called rap jungle jive! True story! That's what drove me to the Scriptures and years later offered y'all Lofty. Dr. Anderson, David Rojas, Mr. Singer, Doug Thigpen. Mrs. Monje and Herrera for turning down my advances. Lol! Would have never met mi Alma. Thank Silvana, Miss Jenna Kamp – the most outside-the-box teachers who knew these kids could learn at risk and didn't buy that at risk rhetoric. Nicolette, the Wilsons, an adopted clan of 12. I witnessed troubled abandoned kids get loved into success! Huizars, Neyda, Dahlia, and Graciella Conchas. I was there when your pop died. I still got that bracelet. Cynthia Saldana. Oh! Patience and both Uplands. Tiffany, Kaamill, Spencer, Masonry, Bianca, Uyen, Nick Luevano, and Raphi Cala. These kids were the fuel for at least three albums. Thank the Blowed. Thank A Mic and Dim Lights, up the street, round the corner where my heart is best kept. Thank Best Kept and Shihan. They're why I love poetry. And the encouragement of my Ate, Irene Fay Duller, to try my hand at poetry. How's Jodel doing?! Thank El Taco Naco, where Taboo of the Black Eyed Peas accidentally kicked me and chipped my front tooth. True story! Thank Zane One and Sareem poems and Ozay Moore. Rosario Ortega, Shames Worthy, James, Janice, Nichole Petty, Thomas Joseph Terry. These deserve your thanks. If you see them, tell them I sent you. I didn't know it then but now I can't ignore. This is my crimson cord. Tell me yours.

ABOUT THE AUTHOR

From the same soil that grew Jim Morrison, Tony Hawk, NWA, Snoop, & Kendrick Lamar, grows another LA native, Propaganda. What do you say about Propaganda? He's a poet, political activist, husband, father, academic, & emcee. With LA flowing through his veins & armed with a bold message, Propaganda has assembled a body of work that challenges his listeners with every verse & reaches across the spectrum of pop culture. From aggressive battle raps to smooth introspective rhythms, Propaganda's music will cause you to nod your head, but more importantly it will stretch your mind & heart.

ABOUT THE PHOTOGRAPHER

Coming from the Bay Area I was exposed to so many different cultures. My upbringing has shaped the way that I view things as an artist. My father was an incredible artist, but worked in tech. My mom was very creative; from them I learned to appreciate art. My parents taught me to paint and sketch, but my true love was photography and cinematography. I became interested at the age of 8. Although I have an extensive commercial background, my passion and expertise is in documentary work. I've always drawn my inspiration from people. My ability to connect with people has allowed me the opportunity to document people from all walks of life in a way that portrays their beauty and inner essence. My goal is to inspire people to look beyond their flaws and encourage them to dream, be free and pursue their God given purpose. My photography has been influenced by Gordon Parks, Ansel Adams, Irving Penn, Richard Avedon and Jonathan Mannion.

ABOUT THE PUBLISHER

Humble Beast is a family of creatives, pastors, writers, theologians, and musicians who leverage their talents to see the Gospel go out into the community and transform lives. We do this as individuals and as a family. Individually, we live our lives as missionaries, disciple-makers, and culture-creators. As a family, we combine our efforts to create a hub of Gospel-saturated resources, communicated in compelling ways and freely shared with everyday people. Humble Beast Records is the home of Propaganda, Beautiful Eulogy, JGivens and Jackie Hill-Perry. Humble Beast is a creative collective of individuals who attempt to express our life through our gifts with our best. What does that look like? Humble Beast is a collective of individuals who share the same commitments & convictions. We strive to live out our lives openly with every person in as many ways as possible. We all share the same open and honest commitment to Jesus Christ. We strive to do all of this with transparency in all humility. Humble Beast is a collective of artists who make music & resources. With each production, Humble Beast aims to be compelling & authentic for our culture. We pour our lives into each of these resources & in turn we give them away for free. Humble Beast is a collective of innovative minds who prize the very best in quality. Everything we do comes from our best efforts, not our leftovers. We strive for excellence & pour everything into what we do at Humble Beast – all for the glory and honor of the One who poured out His life for us, Jesus Christ. Want to support our efforts? Check out our website to find ways that you can partner with us! www.humblebeast.com

DOWNLOAD PROPAGANDA'S MUSIC
FOR FREE AT WWW.HUMBLEBEAST.COM

humble beast.

TELL ME YOURS